MEASUREMENT – TASK & DRILL SHEETS
Principles & Standards of Math Series

• • • • • • • • • • • • • • • • • •

Written by Chris Forest

GRADES 6 – 8

Classroom Complete Press
P.O. Box 19729
San Diego, CA 92159
Tel: 1-800-663-3609 | Fax: 1-800-663-3608
Email: service@classroomcompletepress.com

www.classroomcompletepress.com

ISBN-13: 978-1-55319-547-4

© 2011

Process Standards Rubric

Measurement – Task & Drill Sheets

Measurement – Task Sheets

Expectations — Instructional programs from pre-kindergarten through grade 12 should enable all students to:	1	2	3	4	5	6	7	8	9	10	11	12	13	14	15	Drill Sheet 1	Drill Sheet 2	Review A	Review B	Review C
GOAL 1: Problem Solving • build new mathematical knowledge through problem solving; • solve problems that arise in mathematics and in other contexts; • apply and adapt a variety of appropriate strategies to solve problems; • monitor and reflect on the process of mathematical problem solving.	✓	✓	✓	✓	✓	✓	✓	✓	✓	✓	✓	✓	✓	✓	✓	✓	✓	✓	✓	✓
GOAL 2: Reasoning & Proof • recognize reasoning and proof as fundamental aspects of mathematics; • make and investigate mathematical conjectures; • develop and evaluate mathematical arguments and proofs; • select and use various types of reasoning and methods of proof.	✓		✓	✓	✓	✓		✓	✓	✓	✓	✓	✓		✓	✓	✓	✓	✓
GOAL 3: Communication • organize and consolidate their mathematical thinking through communication; • communicate their mathematical thinking coherently and clearly to peers, teachers, and others; • analyze and evaluate the mathematical thinking and strategies of others; • use the language of mathematics to express mathematical ideas precisely.	✓	✓	✓	✓	✓	✓	✓	✓	✓	✓	✓	✓	✓	✓	✓	✓	✓	✓	✓	✓
GOAL 4: Connections • recognize and use connections among mathematical ideas; • understand how mathematical ideas interconnect and build on one another to produce a coherent whole; • recognize and apply mathematics in contexts outside of mathematics.	✓	✓	✓	✓	✓	✓		✓	✓			✓	✓	✓	✓	✓	✓	✓	✓	✓
GOAL 5: Representation • create and use representations to organize, record, and communicate mathematical ideas; • select, apply, and translate among mathematical representations to solve problems; • use representations to model and interpret physical, social, and mathematical phenomena.	✓		✓	✓	✓	✓			✓	✓	✓	✓	✓	✓	✓	✓	✓	✓	✓	✓

Process Standards Rubric

Measurement – Task & Drill Sheets

Measurement – Drill Sheets

Drills		Warm-up 1	Timed Drill 1	Timed Drill 2	Warm-up 2	Timed Drill 3	Timed Drill 4	Warm-up 3	Timed Drill 5	Timed Drill 6	Warm-up 4	Timed Drill 7	Timed Drill 8	Warm-up 5	Timed Drill 9	Warm-up 6	Timed Drill 10	Timed Drill 11	Review A	Review B	Review C

Expectations
Instructional programs from pre-kindergarten through grade 12 should enable all students to:

GOAL 1: Problem Solving
- build new mathematical knowledge through problem solving;
- solve problems that arise in mathematics and in other contexts;
- apply and adapt a variety of appropriate strategies to solve problems;
- monitor and reflect on the process of mathematical problem solving.

GOAL 2: Reasoning & Proof
- recognize reasoning and proof as fundamental aspects of mathematics;
- make and investigate mathematical conjectures;
- develop and evaluate mathematical arguments and proofs;
- select and use various types of reasoning and methods of proof.

GOAL 3: Communication
- organize and consolidate their mathematical thinking through communication;
- communicate their mathematical thinking coherently and clearly to peers, teachers, and others;
- analyze and evaluate the mathematical thinking and strategies of others;
- use the language of mathematics to express mathematical ideas precisely.

GOAL 4: Connections
- recognize and use connections among mathematical ideas;
- understand how mathematical ideas interconnect and build on one another to produce a coherent whole;
- recognize and apply mathematics in contexts outside of mathematics.

GOAL 5: Representation
- create and use representations to organize, record, and communicate mathematical ideas;
- select, apply, and translate among mathematical representations to solve problems;
- use representations to model and interpret physical, social, and mathematical phenomena.

Measurement – Task & Drill Sheets CC3315

Contents

● ● ● ● ● ● ● ● ● ● ● ● ● ● ● ● ● ●

TEACHER GUIDE

STUDENT HANDOUTS

Measurement – Task Sheets

✔ **6 BONUS** Activity Pages! **Additional worksheets for your students**

FREE!

- Go to our website: **www.classroomcompletepress.com/bonus**
- Enter item CC3115
- Enter pass code CC3115D for Activity Pages.

Contents

✔ **6 BONUS** Activity Pages! **Additional worksheets for your students**

FREE!

- Go to our website: **www.classroomcompletepress.com/bonus**
- Enter item CC3215
- Enter pass code CC3215D for Activity Pages.

NCTM Content Standards Assessment Rubric

Measurement – Task & Drill Sheets

Student's Name: _____ Assignment: _____ Level: _____

	Level 1	Level 2	Level 3	Level 4
Understanding Measurable Attributes of Objects and the Units, Systems, and Processes of Measurement	• Demonstrates a limited understanding of measurable attributes of objects and the units, systems, and processes of measurement	• Demonstrates a basic understanding of measurable attributes of objects and the units, systems, and processes of measurement	• Demonstrates a good understanding of measurable attributes of objects and the units, systems, and processes of measurement	• Demonstrates a thorough understanding of measurable attributes of objects and the units, systems, and processes of measurement
Applying Appropriate Techniques, Tools, and Formulas to Determine Measurements	• Demonstrates limited ability in applying appropriate techniques, tools, and formulas to determine measurements	• Demonstrates some ability in applying appropriate techniques, tools, and formulas to determine measurements	• Demonstrates satisfactory ability in applying appropriate techniques, tools, and formulas to determine measurements	• Demonstrates strong ability in applying appropriate techniques, tools, and formulas to determine measurements

STRENGTHS:

WEAKNESSES:

NEXT STEPS:

Teacher Guide

Our resource has been created for ease of use by both *TEACHERS* and *STUDENTS* alike.

Introduction

The NCTM content standards have been used in the creation of the assignments in this booklet. This method promotes the idea that it is beneficial to learn through practical, applicable, real-world examples. Many of the task and drill sheets are organized around a central problem taken from real-life experiences of the students. The pages of this booklet contain a variety in terms of levels of difficulty and content so as to provide students with a variety of different opportunities. Included are activities on length, width, height, weight, capacity, perimeter, area, surface area, angle measurements, time and money. Visual models are included to assist visual learners. Teachers may also choose to use mathematics manipulatives along with the exercises included in this book to help address the needs of kinesthetic learners.

How Is Our Resource Organized?

STUDENT HANDOUTS

Reproducible **task sheets** and **drill sheets** make up the majority of our resource.

The **task sheets** contain challenging problem-solving tasks in drill form, many centered around 'real-world' ideas or problems, which push the boundaries of critical thought and demonstrate to students why mathematics is important and applicable in the real world. It is not expected that all activities will be used, but are offered for variety and flexibility in teaching and assessment. Many of the drill sheet problems offer space for reflection, and opportunity for the appropriate use of technology, as encouraged by the NCTM's *Principles & Standards for School Mathematics*.

The **drill sheets** contain 11 Timed Drill Sheets and 6 Warm-Up Drill Sheets, featuring real-life problem-solving opportunities. The drill sheets are provided to help students with their procedural proficiency skills, as emphasized by the *NCTM's Curriculum Focal Points*.

The **NCTM Content Standards Assessment Rubric** (*page 6*) is a useful tool for evaluating students' work in many of the activities in our resource. The **Reviews** (*pages 26-28 and 46-48*) are divided by grade and can be used for a follow-up review or assessment at the completion of the unit.

PICTURE CUES

Our resource contains three main types of pages, each with a different purpose and use. A **Picture Cue** at the top of each page shows, at a glance, what the page is for.

 Teacher Guide
* Information and tools for the teacher

 Student Handout
* Reproducible drill sheets

 Easy Marking™ Answer Key
* Answers for student activities

 Timed Drill Stopwatch
* Write the amount of time for students to complete the timed drill sheet in the stopwatch. Recommended times are given on the contents page.

EASY MARKING™ ANSWER KEY

Marking students' worksheets is fast and easy with our **Answer Key**. Answers are listed in columns – just line up the column with its corresponding worksheet, as shown, and see how every question matches up with its answer!

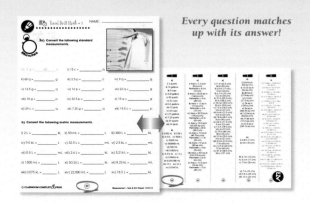

Every question matches up with its answer!

Principles & Standards

Principles & Standards for School Mathematics outlines the essential components of an effective school mathematics program.

The NCTM's Principles & Standards for School Mathematics

The **Principles** are the fundamentals to an effective mathematics education. The **Standards** are descriptions of what mathematics instruction should enable students to learn. Together the **Principles and Standards** offer a comprehensive and coherent set of learning goals, serving as a resource to teachers and a framework for curriculum. Our resource offers exercises written to the NCTM **Process** and **Content Standards** and is inspired by the **Principles** outlined below.

Six Principles for School Mathematics

Equity

EQUITY: All students can learn mathematics when they have access to high-quality instruction, including reasonable and appropriate accommodation and appropriately challenging content.

Curriculum

CURRICULUM: The curriculum must be coherent, focused, and well articulated across the grades, with ideas linked to and building on one another to deepen students' knowledge and understanding.

Teaching

TEACHING: Effective teaching requires understanding what students know and need to learn and then challenging and supporting them to learn it well.

Learning

LEARNING: By aligning factual knowledge and procedural proficiency with conceptual knowledge, students can become effective learners, reflecting on their thinking and learning from their mistakes.

Assessment

ASSESSMENT: The tasks teachers select for assessment convey a message to students about what kinds of knowledge and performance are valued. Feedback promotes goal-setting, responsibility, and independence.

Technology

TECHNOLOGY: Students can develop a deeper understanding of mathematics with the appropriate use of technology, which can allow them to focus on decision-making, reflection, reasoning, and problem solving.

Our resource correlates to the six Principles and provides teachers with supplementary materials, which can aid them in fulfilling the expectations of each principle. The exercises provided allow for variety and flexibility in teaching and assessment. The topical division of concepts and processes promotes linkage and the building of conceptual knowledge and understanding throughout the student's grade and middle school career. Each of the drill sheet problems help students with their procedural proficiency skills, and offers space for reflection and opportunity for the appropriate use of technology.

NAME: _____

Task Sheet 1

Touch The Sky

1) **Stephanie is editing the tenth edition of World's Tallest Buildings. As part of her job, she needs to convert the following heights of the several skyscrapers from feet to meters. Look at the table below and then help her convert the building heights from feet to meters.**

Building	Height in Feet	Height in Meters
Willis Tower	1450 (Chicago)	
Citic Plaza	1283 (China)	
Empire State Building	1250 (New York)	
Central Plaza	1227 (Hong Kong)	
Emirates Tower One	1165 (U.A.E)	
John Hancock Center	1127 (Chicago)	
Chrysler Building	1046 (New York)	
Bank of America Plaza	1023 (Atlanta)	
Library Tower	1018 (Los Angeles)	
Commerzbank Tower	981 (Germany)	

Explore With Technology

Use the Internet to find information about other famous skyscrapers throughout the world. Find three other buildings that could be added to this list above. List the buildings below, and write their height in feet and meters.

Building One: _____

Building Two: _____

Building Three: _____

Task Sheet 2

Scaling Up

2) For this activity you will need a ruler. Either standard or metric will do. With the supervision of an adult, measure the length of seven objects in your classroom. Write the length of each object in the chart below. Then, put your object into a scale that could be used to make a map of your classroom. Use either of the following scales: 1 inch = 1 foot (or 1 cm = 10 cm). So, an object you measured to be 2 feet (60 cm) would be listed on the scale as 2 inches (5 cm).

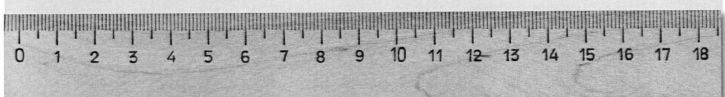

Object	Real Length	Scaled Length
1.		
2.		
3.		
4.		
5.		
6.		
7.		

Reflection

Think about reasons that scales are used in drawings. List three places you might find items that are drawn to scale. Write your thoughts below.

_____

_____

_____

NAME: _____

Task Sheet 3

Angling Around

3) Jared has been trying to draw angles as part of a math challenge activity. His job is to draw the angles described below. Look at the clues carefully. Tell how many degrees each angle is going to have based on the clues you read.

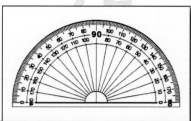

a) **The first angle is a right angle. How many degrees will it have?**

Answer: _____

b) **The second angle is one-third the size of a right angle. How many degrees will it have?**

Answer: _____

c) **The third angle is 25° more than a right angle. How many degrees will it have?**

Answer: _____

d) **The fourth angle is a complementary angle to a 70° angle. How many degrees will it have?**

Answer: _____

e) **The fifth angle is two-thirds the size of a right angle. How many degrees will it have?**

Answer: _____

f) **The sixth angle is a straight angle. How many degrees will it have?**

Answer: _____

g) **The seventh angle is a supplementary angle to a 100° angle. How many degrees will it have?**

Answer: _____

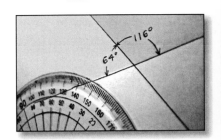
Task Sheet 4

A Protracted Arrangement

4)   For the following activity, you are going to need a protractor. Then, look at the clues in each box. Draw the angle that is being described with the clue. Then, write how many degrees each angle will have.

Angle One: Draw an angle that equals one-half a right angle.

How many degrees is the angle? _____

Angle Two: Draw a supplementary angle to an angle that is 100°.

How many degrees is the angle? _____

Angle Three: Draw a complementary angle to an angle that is 60°.

How many degrees is the angle? _____

Angle Four: Draw an angle that is one-third the size of a 45° angle.

How many degrees is the angle? _____

Angle Five: Draw an angle that equals one and one-half right angles.

How many degrees is the angle? _____

Angle Six: Draw an angle that is 30° less than a straight angle.

How many degrees is the angle? _____

NAME: _____

Task Sheet 5

Volume's Up

5) Anika is in charge of gift wrapping at a local clothing store. As part of her training, she is learning about the different capacity of rectangular boxes that she might use to wrap gifts. She has to complete the table below by telling a possible length, width, and height that could yield each capacity. Complete the table with correct answers Anika might write. Note that the boxes are measured in cubic inches and cubic centimeters.

Box	Possible Length	Possible Width	Possible Height	Capacity
1.				64 cubic inches
2.				120 cubic inches
3.				81 cubic inches
4.				240 cubic inches
5.				150 cubic inches
6.				90 cubic inches
7.				2392 cubic centimeters
8.				2000 cubic centimeters
9.				3600 cubic centimeters
10.				7500 cubic centimeters
11.				2700 cubic centimeters

Explore With Technology

Add three more boxes to this chart, including the length, width, height, and capacity.

Box 12: _____

Box 13: _____

Box 14: _____

Task Sheet 6

Wild Wind Chill

6) The National Meteorological Service helps track wind chill during the winter months. It uses a wind chill scale to help show how wind velocity affects temperature. For example, if the temperature is 35°F (2°C) and the wind is blowing at 15 miles per hour (24 kilometers per hour), the temperature feels like 16°F (-9°C). Use the portion of the wind chill chart below to answer a few of the questions that were asked to the National Meteorological Service.

Wind Speed		Temperature in degrees Fahrenheit (in degrees Celsius)				
		35 (2)	**30 (-1)**	**25 (-4)**	**20 (-7)**	**15 (-9)**
5 mph (8 kph)	feels like	33 (1)	27 (-3)	21 (-6)	19 (-7)	12 (-11)
10 mph (16 kph)		22 (-6)	16 (-9)	10 (-12)	3 (-16)	-3 (-19)
15 mph (24kph)		16 (-9)	9 (-13)	2 (-17)	-5 (-21)	-11 (-24)
20 mph (32kph)		12 (-11)	4 (-16)	-3 (-19)	-10 (-23)	-17 (-27)
25 mph (40kph)		8 (-13)	1 (-17)	-7 (-22)	-15 (-26)	-22 (-30)

a) **According to this chart, how hard must a wind be blowing for a temperature of 20°F (-7°C) to feel like it is -5°F (-21°C)?**

Answer: _____

b) **Which wind speed on this chart shows the smallest affect on a temperature?**

Answer: _____

c) **What is the difference between the affects of a 10 mph (16 kph) wind and a 20 mph (32 kph) wind on a temperature of 20°F (-4°C)?**

Answer: _____

d) **For a 25 mph (40 kph) wind to feel below zero, the air temperature must be at least lower than what temperature?**

Answer: _____

Measurement – Task & Drill Sheets CC3315

NAME: _____

Task Sheet 7

A Certain Area

7) You have been asked to draw a variety of shapes for an updated version of a shape book for children. Your job is to read the directions. Draw each shape based on the dimensions. Then, find the area for each shape after you draw it. To do this, you will need a centimeter ruler.

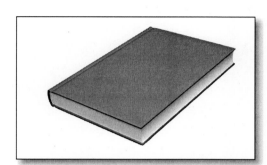

a) Draw a square with each side equal to 4 cm.

Area of shape: _____

b) Draw an equilateral triangle. All sides should equal 3 cm.

Area of shape: _____

c) Draw a rectangle. The length should equal 4 cm. The height should equal 2 cm.

Area of shape: _____

NAME: _____

Task Sheet 8

The Milk Study

8) Jason is studying the change in the price of milk at the end of the year during a seven year period. He is studying the average price per gallon of milk at stores in his neighborhood. Yet, he also wants to convert the price per gallon to the price per quart (or price per liter to the price per 500 milliliter). Help him do this in the chart below.

Year	Price per gallon	Price per quart	Price per liter	Price per 500 milliliter
1	$2.99		$0.79	
2	$3.02		$0.80	
3	$3.08		$0.82	
4	$3.17		$0.84	
5	$3.29		$0.87	
6	$3.44		$0.91	
7	$3.62		$0.96	
8	$3.83		$1.01	

a) **Study the chart carefully above and look for any patterns in how the price changed. Suppose the current rate of price change continued. If you had to predict the price per gallon (or liter) for Year 9 and Year 10, what would the prices of a gallon (or liter) of milk be? How did you determine your answer?**

_____

_____

_____

_____

_____

NAME: _____

Task Sheet 9

Circle Central

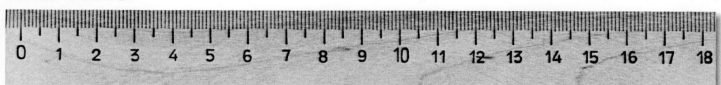

9) For this activity, you will need a compass and a centimeter ruler. Your job is to draw the three circles described below. Then, find the circumference, radius, and area of the circle you draw.

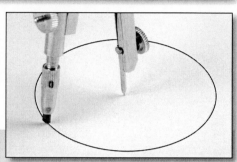

a) **Circle One: Should have a diameter of 2 cm.**

Circumference: _____ Radius: _____ Area: _____

b) **Circle Two:**
Should have a diameter of 3 cm.

Circumference: _____
Radius: _____
Area: _____

c) **Circle Three:**
Should have a diameter of 4 cm.

Circumference: _____
Radius: _____
Area: _____

NAME: _____

Task Sheet 10

Tons, Pounds, and Ounces

10) Tia was making the following chart of items for a science report. She was listing mammals based on their weight in terms of tons, pounds, and ounces. Tia wanted to be sure she listed the weight in each unit to show just how large the mammals were. She was able to find the weight for certain animals in certain measurements. Help her complete the entire chart by calculating the missing information.

Item	Weight in Tons	Weight in Pounds	Weight in Kilograms	Weight in Ounces
Blue Whale	190			
Fin Whale	80			
Right Whale			63,503	
Bowhead Whale				2,080,000
Elephant		15,000		
Hippopotamus	3.5			
Rhinoceros			2,268	
Giraffe		3,000		
Water Buffalo	1.25			
Polar Bear				8,000

Explore With Technology

Using a website or other computer reference tool, look up the difference between a "short ton" and a "long ton." What does each term mean? Why are these two separate terms sometimes used to describe a ton? Write the information you find in the space below.

_____

_____

_____

NAME: _____

Task Sheet 11

It's About the Area

11) For the following project, your job is to select ten objects in your classroom. Use a ruler to measure the perimeter of each object. Then, calculate the area of the object. Make sure to do your measuring with adult supervision.

Object One: _____

Perimeter: _____ **Area:** _____

Object Two: _____

Perimeter: _____ **Area:** _____

Object Three: _____

Perimeter: _____ **Area:** _____

Object Four: _____

Perimeter: _____ **Area:** _____

Object Five: _____

Perimeter: _____ **Area:** _____

Object Six: _____

Perimeter: _____ **Area:** _____

Object Seven: _____

Perimeter: _____ **Area:** _____

Object Eight: _____

Perimeter: _____ **Area:** _____

Object Nine: _____

Perimeter: _____ **Area:** _____

Object Ten: _____

Perimeter: _____ **Area:** _____

Measurement – Task & Drill Sheets CC3315

 Task Sheet

NAME: _____

Task Sheet 12

Dining In

12) Janelle works at the Carroll Café, a small restaurant near her school. The following is a partial copy of the lunch menu found at the restaurant. Use the menu to answer the questions below.

CARROLL CAFÉ - Lunch Menu

Sandwiches	Sides	Beverages
Vegetarian Pocket .. $4.99	Fruit Cup $3.99	Soft Drinks
Meatball Sub $4.99	Salad $3.99	Small $1.00
Cold Cut Sub $5.99	Breadsticks $4.99	Medium .. $1.50
Chicken Cutlet $7.99	Potato Skins ... $5.99	Large $2.00

a) Janelle's first customer ordered a meatball sub, a fruit cup, and a medium soft drink. What was the customer's total before tax?

_____

b) One item on the menu is approximately 1/8 the cost of another item. Name both items.

_____

c) Janelle's second customer ordered a sandwich, a side, and a beverage totaling $15.98 before tax. What three items did the customer order?

_____

d) If a customer ordered a small soft drink, a salad, and a cold cut sub, and there was a 5 percent meal tax on the total, how much would the customer spend in total on the meal?

_____

Explore With Technology   Find out the local meal tax in your location. Write the tax rate below. How does it compare to the rate charged at the Carroll Café?

Task Sheet 13

The Secret Formula

13) Look at the formulas below. Each shows a way of finding the area of plane figures. Determine the figure that is represented by each formula. Then, draw an example of the figure it represents below each formula. Label the length of each side or important line (you may use real lengths by measuring with a ruler or invent your own lengths). Then, determine the area using the information you have written. Some formulas may have more than one correct answer.

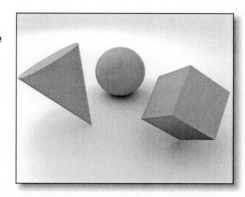

Formula one: $A = \frac{1}{2} b \times h$

Formula two: $A = l \times h$

Formula three: $A = \varpi r^2$

Formula four: $A = s^2$

Reflection Think about the area of the figures determined by formula two and four. If you did not have a formula for these figures, how could formula one and the figure it represents help you determine the area of these two figures?

Task Sheet 14

Turn up the Volume

14) Casey has three solid figures below. He has to determine the volume of each figure, but has never done this before. Help Casey develop a strategy to determine the volume of each figure. Explain what you think would be the best way to determine the volume.

Figure One:

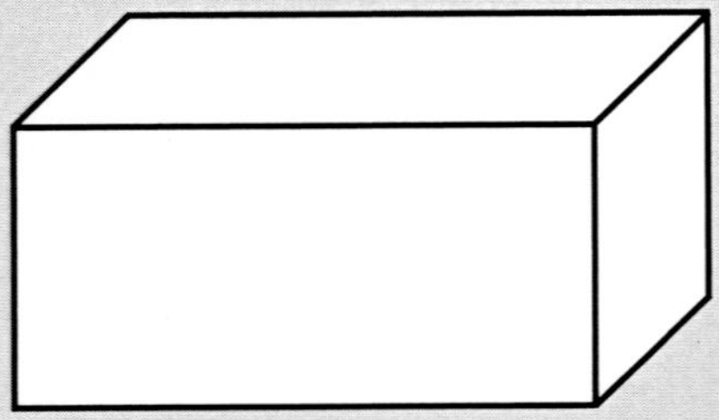

Strategy: _____

_____

_____

_____

_____

_____

Figure Two:

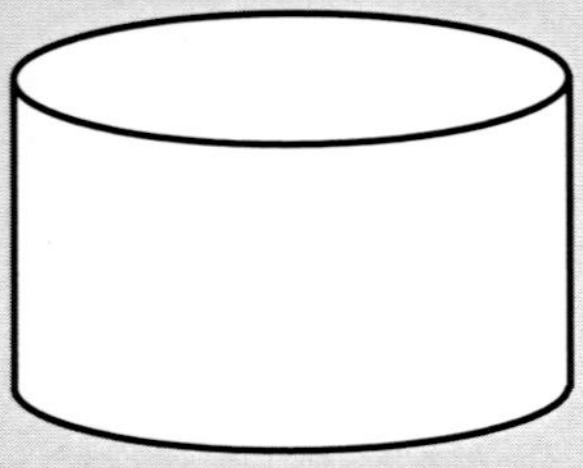

Strategy: _____

_____

_____

_____

_____

_____

Figure Three:

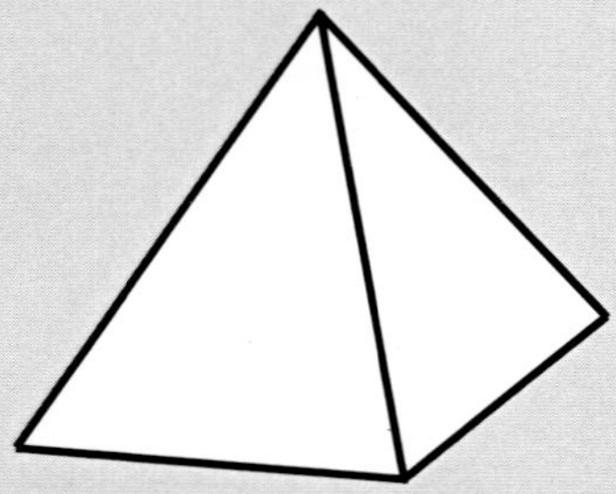

Strategy: _____

_____

_____

_____

_____

_____

Measurement – Task & Drill Sheets CC3315

NAME: _____

Task Sheet 15

Less Dense

15) The formula for calculating density is density = mass divided by volume. Use this formula to complete the table below for the density of cubes used in a science experiment in Ms. Wong's class.

Item	Mass	Volume	Density
Cube 1	10 g (0.35 oz)	12 cm³ (0.73 in³)	g/cm³ (oz/in³)
Cube 2	16 g (0.56 oz)	19 cm³ (1.16 in³)	g/cm³ (oz/in³)
Cube 3	20 g (0.71 oz)	26 cm³ (1.59 in³)	g/cm³ (oz/in³)
Cube 4	22 g (0.78 oz)	28 cm³ (1.71 in³)	g/cm³ (oz/in³)
Cube 5	25 g (0.88 oz)	30 cm³ (1.83 in³)	g/cm³ (oz/in³)
Cube 6	30 g (1.06 oz)	32 cm³ (1.95 in³)	g/cm³ (oz/in³)
Cube 7	32 g (1.13 oz)	40 cm³ (2.44 in³)	g/cm³ (oz/in³)
Cube 8	38 g (1.34 oz)	44 cm³ (2.69 in³)	g/cm³ (oz/in³)
Cube 9	41 g (1.45 oz)	50 cm³ (3.05 in³)	g/cm³ (oz/in³)
Cube 10	45 g (1.59 oz)	52 cm³ (3.17 in³)	g/cm³ (oz/in³)

Explore With Technology

Use computer reference tools and the Internet to research why density is calculated in science experiments. Write two reasons why it is calculated.

Reason 1: _____

_____

_____

Reason 2: _____

_____

_____

Drill Sheet 1

Conversions

a)

1.5 m = _____ cm	27 ft = _____ yards	180 in = _____ ft
2.5 oz = _____ lbs	2.5 g = _____ mg	.25 ton = _____ lbs
4 cups = _____ pints	330 L = _____ kL	2 gallons = _____ quarts
18 ft = _____ yds	2.5 km = _____ m	27 yd = _____ in

Area and Perimeter

Look carefully at the three figures below. Calculate the area and perimeter using the measurements provided.

10 cm

6 cm

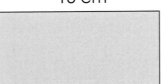

7 in   7 in

3 in

7 in

4 m

b) Area: _____

Perimeter: _____

c) Area: _____

Perimeter: _____

d) Area: _____

Perimeter: _____

Short Answers

e) What is the volume of a tank with a length of 4 feet (1 meter), width of 5 feet (2 meters), and a height of 3 feet (0.9 meters)?

_____

f) What temperature is 20° below the boiling point on the Fahrenheit (Celsius) scale?

_____

g) An angle that is four-fifths the size of a right triangle would be this many degrees.

_____

h) What is the formula for finding the area of a circle?

_____

i) How many meters (feet) are in a 5 km (3 mile) race?

_____

NAME: _____

Drill Sheet 2

Conversions

a)

15 yd = _____ ft	200 mm = _____ cm	90 in = _____ ft
900 g = _____ kg	480 oz = _____ lbs	2 tons = _____ lbs
5 quarts = _____ gallons	8 cups = _____ quarts	160 mL = _____ L
9 km = _____ m	30.5 ft = _____ in	5 m = _____ mm

Angle Measurement

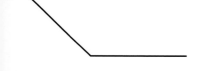

b)   Angle One _____°   **c) Angle One _____°**   **d) Angle One _____°**

Short Answers

e)   What is the area of a square with a side of 5 cm (2 in)?

_____

f)   What portion of a circle is twice as long as the radius?

_____

g)   If a house has an area of 25 sq. ft (2 sq. m) on a floor plan and the scale is 1:10, how big is the house?

_____

h)   What is the perimeter of an equilateral triangle with a base of 5 inches (13 cm)?

_____

i)   Jonathan travels a distance of 150 miles (241 kilometers) by bicycle. He travels for six consecutive days, traveling the same amount of miles (kilometers) each day. How many miles (kilometers) does he travel in two days?

_____

Review A

Measurement Conversions

a) 10,560 feet = _____ inches _____ yd _____ miles

6000 m = _____ mm _____ cm _____ km

1000 lbs = _____ oz _____ tons

16 quarts = _____ cups _____ pints _____ gallons

Measurement

b) Draw the three figures described below. You may use a centimeter ruler and protractor or other measurement devices to help you.

Figure 1: a square with a perimeter of 10 cm (4 in)

Figure 2: an angle that measures 100°

Figure 3: a triangle with a base of 1 inch (3 cm)

Open response

c) Using two to five sentences, explain how you would find the area and perimeter of a rectangle. You may draw a diagram below to help explain your response.

_____

_____

_____

_____

_____

NAME: _____

Review B

Conversions

a) 2.5 miles = _____ inches _____ ft _____ yd

3.5 km = _____ mm _____ cm _____ m

4 tons = _____ oz _____ lbs

5 gallons = _____ cups _____ pints _____ quarts

Measurement

b) Draw the three figures described below. You may use a centimeter ruler and protractor or other measurement devices to help you.

Figure 1: a rectangle with an area of 20 sq. cm (3 sq. in)

Figure 2: an angle that measures 65°

Figure Three: a circle with a radius of 2 cm (0.8 in)

Open response

c) Using two to five sentences, explain how you would find the volume of a rectangular prism. You may draw a diagram below to help explain your response.

_____

_____

_____

_____

_____

Measurement – Task & Drill Sheets CC3315

Review C

Conversions

a) .7 mile = _____ inches _____ ft _____ yd

3500 cm = _____ mm _____ m _____ km

16000 oz = _____ lbs _____ tons

16 cups = _____ pints _____ quarts _____ gallons

Measurement

b) Draw the three figures described below. You may use a centimeter ruler and protractor or other measurement devices to help you.

Figure 1: a circle with a diameter of 1 inch (3 cm)

Figure 2: an angle that measures 155°

Figure 3: a pyramid with a base of 3.5 cm (1 in)

Open response

c) Using two to five sentences, explain how you would find the surface area of a cylinder. You may draw a diagram below to help explain your response.

_____

_____

_____

_____

_____

NAME: _____

1a) Using the information in the menu below, create a list of food or drink combinations and list them in the table. Each combination should have three different items. Then, list the total cost for the combination, including a 5% sales tax. Finally, List the amount of change you would get back if you paid each meal with $10.00.

Fire Station Grill Breakfast Menu			
Bacon (3 strips) = $1.99	Cereal = $2.50	Hash browns = $1.99	Coffee (cup) = $1.50
Sausage (2 links) = $1.50	Oatmeal = $2.99	Fried hash = $2.99	Tea (cup) = $1.50
Eggs (2) = $2.00	Pancakes (3) = $3.00	Cornbread = $1.99	Milk = $1.00
Toast (2 slices) = $1.50	Waffles (2) = $3.00	Muffin = $1.99	Juice = $1.99

Combo	Cost + 5% Sales Tax	Change from $10.00
Ex: Oatmeal, Pancakes, and Muffin	$8.38	$1.62
i)		
ii)		
iii)		
iv)		
v)		
vi)		
vii)		
viii)		
ix)		
x)		

Timed Drill Sheet # 1   NAME: _____

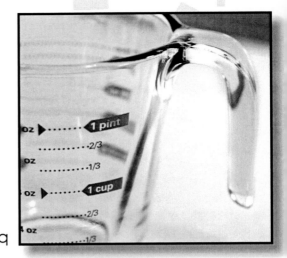

2a) Convert the following standard measurements.

Ex: 5 g = ___40___ p   i) 12 c = _____ q

ii) 60 q = _____ g   iii) 2.5 p = _____ c   iv) 9 q = _____ g

v) 12.5 g = _____ q   vi) 16 p = _____ c   vii) 22 q = _____ g

viii) 18 g = _____ p   ix) 32.5 p = _____ c   x) 15 q = _____ g

xi) 29 c = _____ q   xii) 7.25 g = _____ q   xiii) 19.5 c = _____ p

b) Convert the following metric measurements.

i) 2 L = _____ kL   ii) 50 mL = _____ L   iii) 300 L = _____ kL

iv) 9.5 kL = _____ L   v) 32.5 L = _____ mL   vi) 2.5 kL = _____ mL

vii) 0.5 L = _____ mL   viii) 2.6 L = _____ kL   ix) 5,216 L = _____ kL

x) 1300 mL = _____ L   xi) 50.26 L = _____ kL   xii) 8.23 kL = _____ mL

xiii) 0.075 kL = _____ L   xiv) 22,000 mL = _____ L   xv) 18.5 L = _____ kL

Measurement – Task & Drill Sheets CC3315

3a) Look at the shapes below. The sides of each shape are given. Provide the area and perimeter for each shape.

Ex:

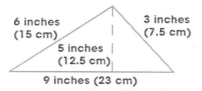

6 inches (15 cm)
3 inches (7.5 cm)
5 inches (12.5 cm)
9 inches (23 cm)

Area = **22.5 sq in (143.75 sq cm)**
Perimeter = **18 in (45.5 cm)**

i)

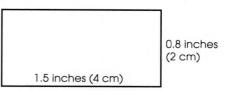

0.8 inches (2 cm)
1.5 inches (4 cm)

Area = _____
Perimeter = _____

ii)

4.5 inches (12 cm)

Area = _____
Perimeter = _____

iii)

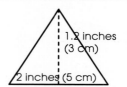

1.2 inches (3 cm)
2 inches (5 cm)

Area = _____
Perimeter = _____

iv)

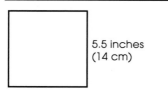

5.5 inches (14 cm)

Area = _____
Perimeter = _____

v)

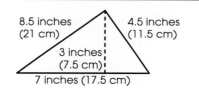

8.5 inches (21 cm)
4.5 inches (11.5 cm)
3 inches (7.5 cm)
7 inches (17.5 cm)

Area = _____
Perimeter = _____

vi)

2.5 inches (6.5 cm)
3 inches (7.5 cm)

Area = _____
Perimeter = _____

vii)

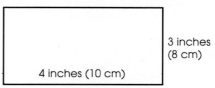

3 inches (8 cm)
4 inches (10 cm)

Area = _____
Perimeter = _____

viii)

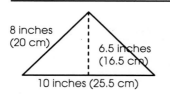

8 inches (20 cm)
6.5 inches (16.5 cm)
10 inches (25.5 cm)

Area = _____
Perimeter = _____

ix)

3 inches (8 cm)
4.5 inches (12 cm)

Area = _____
Perimeter = _____

Measurement – Task & Drill Sheets CC3315

Warm-Up Drill Sheet # 2   NAME: _____

4a) Look at the chart below. It shows the measurements of the sides of a triangle. Determine the perimeter of each triangle. Then, find the perimeter of each triangle if the measurements of each side are doubled.

Triangle	Side 1	Side 2 (base)	Side 3	Height	Perimeter	Perimeter if sizes are doubled
i)	3 in (7.5 cm)	6 in (15 cm)	8 in (20 cm)	4 in (10 cm)		
ii)	1.5 in (4 cm)	3.5 in (9 cm)	1.5 in (4 cm)	2.8 in (7 cm)		
iii)	2 in (5 cm)	1.3 in (3 cm)	2.8 in (7 cm)	2 in (5 cm)		
iv)	2 in (5 cm)	7 in (17.8 cm)	12 in (30.5 cm)	8 in (20 cm)		
v)	2.8 in (7 cm)	5 in (12.5 cm)	2.5 in (6 cm)	4.3 in (11 cm)		
vi)	2.5 in (6 cm)	1.5 in (4 cm)	3.3 in (8.5 cm)	1.8 in (4.5 cm)		
vii)	2.2 in (5.5 cm)	1.5 in (4 cm)	4.7 in (12 cm)	3.7 in (9.5 cm)		
viii)	3 in (7.5 cm)	7 in (17.8 cm)	8 in (20 cm)	3 in (7.5 cm)		
ix)	1 in (2.5 cm)	2.5 in (6 cm)	1.3 in (3 cm)	3 in (7.5 cm)		
x)	1.5 in (4 cm)	3.3 in (8.5 cm)	2.5 in (6 cm)	3.2 in (8 cm)		
xi)	3 in (7.5 cm)	6 in (15 cm)	10 in (25.5 cm)	5 in (12.5 cm)		
xii)	1.5 in (4 cm)	3.7 in (9.5 cm)	4.7 in (12 cm)	3.5 in (9 cm)		
xiii)	3.5 in (9 cm)	1.8 in (4.5 cm)	3.2 in (8 cm)	2.5 in (6 cm)		
xiv)	3 in (7.5 cm)	7.5 in (19 cm)	3 in (7.5 cm)	5 in (12.5 cm)		
xv)	6 in (15 cm)	9 in (23 cm)	12 in (30.5 cm)	5 in (12.5 cm)		

Reflection Redo the activity above by finding the area of each triangle. Then, find the area of each triangle if the measurements of each side and height are doubled.

5a) Determine the surface area for each cube below.
Note: cubes are not to scale.   Formula: Surface Area = $6a^2$

Ex: 1.5 in (3.8 cm)

Surface Area = 6 × (1.5)² = 13.5 sq. in
(Surface Area = 6 × (3.8)² = 86.64 sq. cm)

i)  1.2 in (3 cm)

Surface Area = _____

ii) 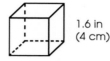 1.6 in (4 cm)

Surface Area = _____

iii) 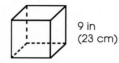 9 in (23 cm)

Surface Area = _____

iv)  1 in (2.5 cm)

Surface Area = _____

v) 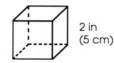 2 in (5 cm)

Surface Area = _____

vi) 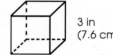 3 in (7.6 cm)

Surface Area = _____

vii)  4.7 in (12 cm)

Surface Area = _____

viii) 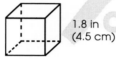 1.8 in (4.5 cm)

Surface Area = _____

ix) 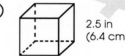 2.5 in (6.4 cm)

Surface Area = _____

b) Draw and label the sides of a cube with the following surface areas.
Note: Drawings do not have to be to scale.

Ex: 24 sq. in (150 sq. cm)   i)   47.04 sq. in (294 sq. cm)   ii)   96 sq. in (600 sq. cm)

 2 in (5 cm)

iii)   132.54 sq. in (864 sq. cm)   iv)   110.94 sq. in (726 sq. cm)   v)   374.46 sq. in (2400 sq. cm)

vi)   294 sq. in (1944 sq. cm)   vii)   576.24 sq. in (3750 sq. cm) viii)   1014 sq. in (6534 sq. cm)

Measurement – Task & Drill Sheets CC3315

6a) Convert the following lengths into two new measurements.

Ex: 92 feet = ___1104___ inches ___0.017___ miles

i)	2.5 miles =	_____ feet	_____ inches
ii)	8250 inches =	_____ feet	_____ miles
iii)	10,000 feet =	_____ miles	_____ inches
iv)	26.2 miles =	_____ feet	_____ inches
v)	22,500 inches =	_____ miles	_____ feet
vi)	12,580 feet =	_____ miles	_____ inches
vii)	27.4 miles =	_____ feet	_____ inches
viii)	82.5 m =	_____ cm	_____ mm
ix)	18.3 km =	_____ m	_____ cm
x)	156 cm =	_____ m	_____ mm
xi)	1258 m =	_____ km	_____ cm
xii)	8276.7 mm =	_____ m	_____ cm
xiii)	413.7 m =	_____ cm	_____ mm
xiv)	92.5 km =	_____ m	_____ cm
xv)	275.5 cm =	_____ m	_____ mm
xvi)	328.5 m =	_____ km	_____ cm
xvii)	23,000 feet =	_____ miles	_____ inches
xviii)	97 miles =	_____ inches	_____ feet
xix)	0.03 km =	_____ cm	_____ m
xx)	250,000 mm =	_____ m	_____ cm

Explore With Technology

Using the Internet, determine how to convert 1 mile into kilometers. Write the formula, then find out how many kilometers are in a mile.

7a) **The diameter or radius of each circle is given. Determine the area and circumference of each circle shown. Note: circles are not to scale.**

Formulas: Area = π radius² Circumference = 2π radius or π diameter (π = 3.14)

Ex:  0.4 in (1 cm)

Area = 0.13 sq in (0.79 sq cm)
Circumference = 1.26 in (3.14cm)

i)  4.7 in (12 cm)

Area = _____
Circumference = _____

ii)  3 in (7.5 cm)

Area = _____
Circumference = _____

iii) 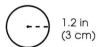 1.2 in (3 cm)

Area = _____
Circumference = _____

iv) 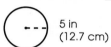 5 in (12.7 cm)

Area = _____
Circumference = _____

v)  6.7 in (17 cm)

Area = _____
Circumference = _____

vi) 3.5 in (9 cm)

Area = _____
Circumference = _____

vii)  10 in (25.5 cm)

Area = _____
Circumference = _____

viii) 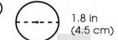 1.8 in (4.5 cm)

Area = _____
Circumference = _____

ix)  7.3 in (18.5 cm)

Area = _____
Circumference = _____

x)  7.5 in (19 cm)

Area = _____
Circumference = _____

xi)  8.9 in (22.5 cm)

Area = _____
Circumference = _____

xii)  1 in (2.5 cm)

Area = _____
Circumference = _____

xiii)  4.5 in (11.5 cm)

Area = _____
Circumference = _____

xiv)  23 in (58.5 cm)

Area = _____
Circumference = _____

xv) 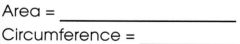 6 in (15.3 cm)

Area = _____
Circumference = _____

xvi)  2 in (5 cm)

Area = _____
Circumference = _____

xvii) 7 in (17.8 cm)

Area = _____
Circumference = _____

Reflection Redo the activity above by finding the area and circumference of each circle if the provided radius and diameter were doubled.

Measurement – Task & Drill Sheets CC3315

NAME: _____

8a) The chart below shows the finishing times of 10 racers in a 4 mile (6.5 km) race. Write the average times in minutes and seconds that it took each racer to complete 1 mile (1.6 km) of the 4 mile (6.5 km) race.

Place	Person	Time	Place	Person	Time
Ex:	Amanda	19.10 min	8	Albert	20.52 min
1	Dorothy	19.25 min	9	Danny	20.75 min
2	Chen	19.75 min	10	Ariel	20.99 min
3	Amie	19.95 min	11	Sara	21.12 min
4	Diego	20.21 min	12	Ashley	22.30 min
5	Stefano	20.45 min	13	Justin	22.35 min
6	Janine	20.46 min	14	Tyler	22.49 min
7	Jonathon	20.48 min	15	Susan	23.01 min

	Person	Minutes per 1 mile (1.6 km)	Seconds per 1 mile (1.6 km)
Ex:	Amanda	4.78 (2.94)	0.08 (0.049)
i)	Dorothy		
ii)	Chen		
iii)	Amie		
iv)	Diego		
v)	Stefano		
vi)	Janine		
vii)	Jonathon		
viii)	Albert		
ix)	Danny		
x)	Ariel		
xi)	Sara		
xii)	Ashley		
xiii)	Justin		
xiv)	Tyler		
xv)	Susan		

NAME: _____

9a) Listed below in the first column are the formulas that are used to determine the area, surface area, or perimeter of different shapes. Write the shape that each formula represents in the second column. Then, using a ruler, draw a sample of each shape using inches or centimeters. Determine the area or perimeter for each shape you draw.

Formula	Shape it may represent	Sample Shape	Area	Perimeter
Ex: P = 4 side	Square		A = s² A = (0.8 in/2 cm)² A = 0.64 sq. in/ 4 sq. cm	P = 4 (0.8 in/2 cm) P = 3.2 in/8 cm
i) A = ½ b x h				
ii) P = 3s				
iii) A = l x w				
iv) P = 5s				
v) A = π r²				
vi) P = 2l + 2w				
vii) A = s²				
viii) P = 6s				
ix) A = 6a²				

10a) **Draw the following shapes described below using a ruler. Then, find the perimeter and area of the shape you have drawn.**

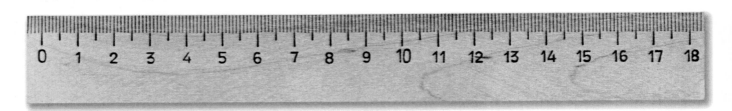

i) A square with a side of 1.3 in (3 cm).

ii) A rectangle with a length of
0.8 in (2 cm) and a width of 1.3 in (3 cm).

Perimeter: _____

Area: _____

Perimeter: _____

Area: _____

iii) A square with sides all equal to
1 in (2.5 cm).

iv) A parallelogram with all sides
equal to 1.3 in (3 cm) and a height
of 0.9 in (2.3 cm).

Perimeter: _____

Area: _____

Perimeter: _____

Area: _____

v) An equilateral triangle with a side
of 0.8 in (2 cm) and a height
of 0.7 in (1.7 cm)

vi) A rectangle with a length
of 1.6 in (4 cm) and a width
of 1 in (2.5 cm).

Perimeter: _____

Area: _____

Perimeter: _____

Area: _____

vii) An isosceles triangle with two
congruent sides of your choice and
height of your choice.

viii) A rectangle where the length
is 2 times the width. You may choose
the measurements.

Perimeter: _____

Area: _____

Perimeter: _____

Area: _____

Minutes

11a) The volume of different packing boxes is listed in the chart below. Determine a possible length, width, and height for each box listed.

Ace Packing Company Box Dimensions

Box	Volume	Length	Width	Height
Ex:	**10 cubic in (158.75 cubic cm)**	2 in (5 cm)	5 in (12.7 cm)	1 in (2.5 cm)
i)	18 cubic in (295 cubic cm)			
ii)	1.5 cubic in (24 cubic cm)			
iii)	2 cubic in (36 cubic cm)			
iv)	9 cubic in (147.5 cubic cm)			
v)	3 cubic in (47 cubic cm)			
vi)	4 cubic in (64 cubic cm)			
vii)	48 cubic in (786.5 cubic cm)			
viii)	6.5 cubic in (105 cubic cm)			
ix)	7.5 cubic in (120 cubic cm)			
x)	140 cubic in (2294 cubic cm)			
xi)	9.5 cubic in (160 cubic cm)			
xii)	13.5 cubic in (220 cubic cm)			
xiii)	99 cubic in (1622 cubic cm)			
xiv)	23 cubic in (380 cubic cm)			
xv)	13 cubic in (210 cubic cm)			
xvi)	60 cubic in (983 cubic cm)			
xvii)	6 cubic in (99 cubic cm)			
xviii)	14.5 cubic in (240 cubic cm)			
xix)	12 cubic in (196.5 cubic cm)			
xx)	31 cubic in (508 cubic cm)			

12a) Convert the following measurements.

i) 12 feet = _____ inches

ii) 0.5 yard = _____ feet

iii) 72 inches = _____ yards

iv) 7.5 feet = _____ yards

v) 2.5 yards= _____ inches

vi) 21 feet = _____ inches

vii) 78 inches = _____ feet

viii) 30 yards = _____ inches

ix) 3.3 yards = _____ inches

x) 42 inches = _____ feet

xi) 16 inches = _____ feet

xii) 26.5 yards = _____ feet

xiii) 3 meters = _____ mm

xiv) 2.5 cm = _____ mm

xv) 19 cm = _____ mm

xvi) 14 meters = _____ cm

xvii) 855 mm = _____ meters

xviii) 9.5 cm = _____ meters

xix) 326 mm = _____ cm

xx) 29 cm = _____ mm

xxi) 25 cm = _____ meters

xxii) 1890 mm = _____ cm

Explore With Technology

Using an online site, determine how to convert inches to centimeters. What is the formula? How would you convert six inches into centimeters? How would you convert 12 centimeters into inches?

Measurement – Task & Drill Sheets CC3315

13a) The chart below shows the dimensions of take-out boxes in a restaurant. Complete the chart by determining the surface area of each box.

Formula: Surface Area = 2(ab) + 2(ac) + 2(bc)
a = height   b = width   c = length

Box	Length	Width	Height	Surface Area
Ex:	6 in (15 cm)	8 in (20 cm)	3 in (7.5 cm)	180 sq. in (1,125 sq. cm)
i)	1 in (2.5 cm)	3 in (7.5 cm)	2 in (5 cm)	
ii)	8 in (20 cm)	5 in (12.5 cm)	4 in (10 cm)	
iii)	12 in (30 cm)	4 in (10 cm)	3 in (7.5 cm)	
iv)	6 in (15 cm)	4.5 in (12 cm)	3 in (7.5 cm)	
v)	12 in (30 cm)	5 in (12.5 cm)	6 in (15 cm)	
vi)	0.5 in (1 cm)	1.5 in (4 cm)	2 in (5 cm)	
vii)	13 in (33 cm)	18 in (45.5 cm)	15 in (38 cm)	
viii)	3 in (7.5 cm)	1.5 in (4 cm)	2 in (5 cm)	
ix)	17 in (43 cm)	13 in (33 cm)	6 in (15 cm)	
x)	9 in (23 cm)	5 in (12.5 cm)	7.5 in (19 cm)	
xi)	10 in (25 cm)	6 in (15 cm)	3 in (7.5 cm)	
xii)	6 in (15 cm)	5 in (12.5 cm)	6 in (15 cm)	
xiii)	8 in (20 cm)	4 in (10 cm)	10 in (25 cm)	
xiv)	4 in (10 cm)	2 in (5 cm)	3 in (7.5 cm)	
xv)	13 in (33 cm)	6 in (15 cm)	5.5 in (14 cm)	
xvi)	1.5 in (4 cm)	5.5 in (14 cm)	2.5 in (6 cm)	
xvii)	1 in (2.5 cm)	0.5 in (1 cm)	1.5 in (4 cm)	
xviii)	17.5 in (45 cm)	3 in (7.5 cm)	6 in (15 cm)	
xix)	7.5 in (19 cm)	3.5 in (8.5 cm)	6 in (15 cm)	
xx)	5 in (12.5 cm)	8.5 in (21.5 cm)	5 in (12.5 cm)	

Timed Drill Sheet # 9

NAME: _____

14a) **The calendar below shows the daily high and low temperatures in Carver City for a five day period in July. Read the information, then answer the questions that follow.**

8 Minutes

Monday	Tuesday	Wednesday	Thursday	Friday
High: 75.6°F (24.2°C) Low: 58.3°F (14.6°C)	High: 77.2°F (25.1°C) Low: 56.8°F (13.8°C)	High: 77.9°F (25.5°C) Low: 52.5°F (11.4°C)	High: 78.4°F (25.8°C) Low: 60.3°F (15.7°C)	High: 72.7°F (22.6°C) Low: 54.8°F (12.7°C)

i) Calculate the difference between the high and low temperatures for each day.

Day:	Monday	Tuesday	Wednesday	Thursday	Friday
Difference:					

ii) What is the average high for the week? _____

iii) What is the average low for the week? _____

iv) What is the mean temperature for each day?

Day:	Monday	Tuesday	Wednesday	Thursday	Friday
Mean:					

v) What day has the greatest difference between high and low? _____

vi) What day has the smallest difference between high and low? _____

vii) What is the difference between the highest and lowest temperature during the week?

_____

Explore With Technology Find the high and low temperatures for the previous week for your own city and fill out the chart below accordingly.

Day:	Monday	Tuesday	Wednesday	Thursday	Friday
High:					
Low:					
Difference:					
Mean:					

15a) Use a ruler to draw the following plane figure (or 2 dimensional) shapes for each perimeter given. For each perimeter, draw 3 different shapes that equal that measurement.

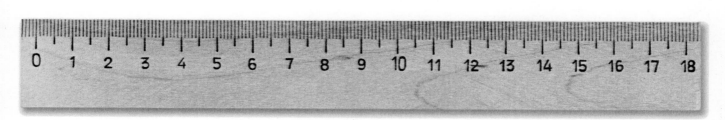

i) Perimeter = 2 inches
Shape 1   Shape 2   Shape 3

ii) Perimeter = 2.5 inches
Shape 1   Shape 2   Shape 3

iii) Perimeter = 3 inches
Shape 1   Shape 2   Shape 3

iv) Perimeter = 4 inches
Shape 1   Shape 2   Shape 3

v) Perimeter = 5 inches
Shape 1   Shape 2   Shape 3

vi) Perimeter = 4.5 inches
Shape 1   Shape 2   Shape 3

16a) The table below shows the measurements between cities on a map. The scale for the map is 1 inch = 25 miles (1 cm = 16 km). Write the number of miles (km) that are located between the two cities in the fourth column.

	Start City	End City	Measurement (in/cm)	Actual Miles/Km
Ex:	Hamilton	Carsonville	1.5 inches (3.8 cm)	37.5 miles (60.8 km)
i)	Hamilton	Marlboro	1.75 inches (4.5 cm)	
ii)	Hamilton	Manchester	2.25 inches (5.7 cm)	
iii)	Carsonville	Wooddale	2.5 inches (6.4 cm)	
iv)	Carsonville	Marlboro	2.75 inches (7 cm)	
v)	Carsonville	East Lehigh	3.25 inches (8.3 cm)	
vi)	Manchester	Marlboro	3.5 inches (8.9 cm)	
vii)	Manchester	Wooddale	3.75 inches (9.5 cm)	
viii)	Manchester	Sun City	4 inches (10.2 cm)	
ix)	Marlboro	Wooddale	4.15 inches (10.5 cm)	
x)	Marlboro	Sun City	4.25 inches (10.8 cm)	
xi)	Marlboro	Paradise Valley	4.5 inches (11.4 cm)	
xii)	Paradise Valley	East Lehigh	4.75 inches (12 cm)	
xiii)	Paradise Valley	Sun City	5 inches (12.7 cm)	
xiv)	Paradise Valley	Silicon	5.2 inches (13.2 cm)	
xv)	Silicon	Marlboro	5.5 inches (14 cm)	
xvi)	Silicon	Sun City	5.75 inches (14.6 cm)	
xvii)	Silicon	Carsonville	6.2 inches (15.8 cm)	
xviii)	Sun City	Wooddale	6.25 inches (15.9 cm)	
xix)	Sun City	East Lehigh	6.75 inches (17.2 cm)	
xx)	Sun City	Albertville	7.5 inches (19 cm)	

NAME: _____

17a) Find the volume and surface area of each box below using the provided measurements.
Note: measurements are not to scale.

i)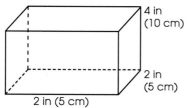

4 in (10 cm)
2 in (5 cm)
2 in (5 cm)

Surface Area = _____

Volume = _____

ii)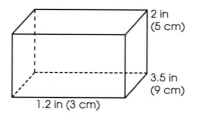

2 in (5 cm)
3.5 in (9 cm)
1.2 in (3 cm)

Surface Area = _____

Volume = _____

iii)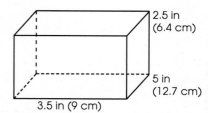

2.5 in (6.4 cm)
5 in (12.7 cm)
3.5 in (9 cm)

Surface Area = _____

Volume = _____

iv)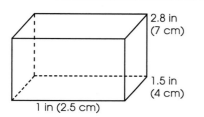

2.8 in (7 cm)
1.5 in (4 cm)
1 in (2.5 cm)

Surface Area = _____

Volume = _____

v)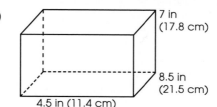

7 in (17.8 cm)
8.5 in (21.5 cm)
4.5 in (11.4 cm)

Surface Area = _____

Volume = _____

vi)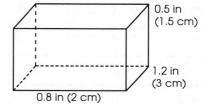

0.5 in (1.5 cm)
1.2 in (3 cm)
0.8 in (2 cm)

Surface Area = _____

Volume = _____

vii)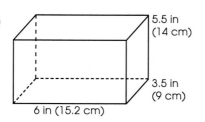

5.5 in (14 cm)
3.5 in (9 cm)
6 in (15.2 cm)

Surface Area = _____

Volume = _____

viii)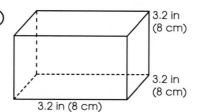

3.2 in (8 cm)
3.2 in (8 cm)
3.2 in (8 cm)

Surface Area = _____

Volume = _____

ix)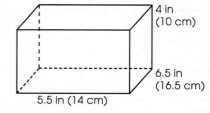

4 in (10 cm)
6.5 in (16.5 cm)
5.5 in (14 cm)

Surface Area = _____

Volume = _____

x)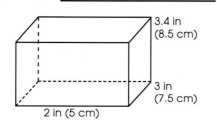

3.4 in (8.5 cm)
3 in (7.5 cm)
2 in (5 cm)

Surface Area = _____

Volume = _____

xi)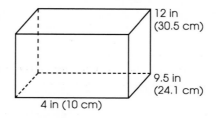

12 in (30.5 cm)
9.5 in (24.1 cm)
4 in (10 cm)

Surface Area = _____

Volume = _____

xii)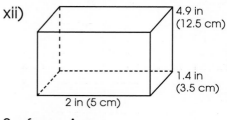

4.9 in (12.5 cm)
1.4 in (3.5 cm)
2 in (5 cm)

Surface Area = _____

Volume = _____

NAME: _____

Review A

a) Convert the following measurements.

i) 20 ft = _____ in   ii) 480 mm = _____ cm   iii) 176 oz = _____ lbs

iv) 500 m = _____ km   v) 72 ft = _____ yd   vi) 7.5 kL = _____ L

vii) 128 qts = _____ gallons   viii) 2.5 m = _____ cm   ix) 45 ft = _____ yd

x) 7 km = _____ mm   xi) 4.5 cup = _____ pt   xii) 12 L = _____ mL

xiii) 18.5 ft = _____ in   xiv) 29. 7 g = _____ mg   xv) 25 lbs = _____ oz

b) Answer the following quick measurement questions.

i) Jaime measured the temperature of a warm liquid. The temperature started at 72°F (22°C) and dropped 2.5 degrees every minute for three minutes. What was the temperature of the liquid after 3 minutes? _____

ii) A rectangle had an area of 2.5 square inches (16 square cm). What are two possible combinations for the length and width of the rectangle?

_____

iii) Tyrone ran a 5 mile (8 km) race. How many total feet (meters) did he run?

_____

iv) If a car weighs 2.5 tons, how many pounds (kilograms) does it weigh?

_____

v) A triangle has a base of 6 inches (150 mm) and a height of 1 inch (25.5 mm). What is the area of the triangle? _____

vi) What is the perimeter of a square with a side measuring 3.5 inches (9 cm)?

_____

c) Use a ruler to measure the objects below. Find the area for each object.

i)
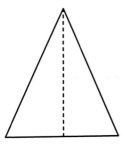

ii)

iii)

Area = _____   Area = _____   Area = _____

NAME: _____

Review B

a) Convert the following measurements.

i) 2.57 cm = _____ mm

ii) 4.5 ft = _____ in

iii) 12.5 gal = _____ cups

iv) 5.5 km = _____ cm

v) 24 oz = _____ lbs

vi) 0.5 kL = _____ L

vii) 138 in = _____ ft

viii) 175 mm = _____ cm

ix) 30 qt = _____ gallons

x) 19.27 mg = _____ g

xi) 28.5 oz = _____ lbs

xii) 29.25 kg = _____ g

xiii) 22.5 ft = _____ in

xiv) 0.025 kL = _____ L

xv) 2.5 tons = _____ oz

b) Answer the following quick measurement questions.

i) Carlos measured the temperature on a cold winter day at -3°F. What was the temperature in Celsius? _____

ii) A regular pentagon has a perimeter of 12 inches (30.5 cm). What is the measure of each side? _____

iii) Dionne weighed herself and determined she was 85.25 pounds (38.67 kilograms). How many ounces (grams) did she weigh? _____

iv) Wan took a car trip with his family. They traveled close to 158.5 miles (255 km) before arriving at their destination after three days. What was the average amount of miles (km) they traveled each day? _____

v) A box has a length of 3 inches (8 cm), width of 2 inches (5 cm), and a height of 2.5 inches (7 cm). What is the volume of the box? _____

c) Use a ruler to measure the objects below. Find the perimeter or circumference for each object.

i)

Perimeter = _____

ii)

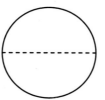

Circumference = _____

iii)

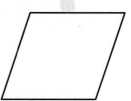

Perimeter = _____

NAME: _____

Review C

a) Convert the following measurements.

i) 18.3 yd = _____ ft   ii) 1.28 cm = _____ mm   iii) 0.25 tons = _____ lbs

iv) 1.025 m = _____ mm   v) 198 oz = _____ lbs   vi) 7.5 g = _____ kg

vii) 144 qt = _____ gal   viii) 1.25 km = _____ cm   ix) 40.3 ft = _____ in

x) 27.55 kg = _____ g   xi) 24.5 ft = _____ yds   xii) 4.25 km = _____ m

xiii) 25.25 g = _____ mg   xiv) 8.25 ft = _____ in   xv) 0.028 kL = _____ L

b) Answer the following quick measurement questions.

i) Steven measured the length of time it took for a science experiment to be completed. After three trials, his times were 18.25 seconds, 16.75 seconds, and 15.27 seconds. What was the average time for the experiments to be completed?

_____

ii) A parallelogram has an area of 4.2 sq. in (27 sq. cm). What are two possible base and height measurements? _____

iii) Diego rode a bike for three consecutive days. He averaged 25.25 miles (40.6 km) each day. How many total feet (meters) had he traveled after three days?

_____

iv) A rectangular box has a length of 3 inches (8 cm), a width of 2 inches (5 cm), and a height of 0.8 inches (2 cm). What is the surface area?

_____

v) The radius of a circle is 5 inches (12.5 cm). What is the area of the circle?

_____

c) Use a ruler to measure the objects below. Find the area, perimeter and circumference for each object.

i)
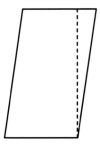

ii)
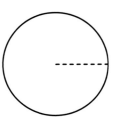

iii)
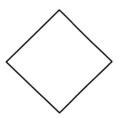

Area = _____   Area = _____   Area = _____

Perimeter = _____   Circumference = _____   Perimeter = _____

7.

Drawings may vary.

a) Area should =
16 sq. cm.

b) Area may vary
depending on height
students choose. The
answer should be
close to 3 – 5 sq. cm.

c) Area should =
8 sq. cm.

(15)

6.

a) 15 mph (24 kph)

b) 5 mph (8 kph)
winds. There is a 21
degrees difference
between effects at
35°F (2°C) and 15°F
(-9°C)

c) There is a 13
degree difference.

d) Students might
have to estimate
this answer. Students
should see that the
temperature must be
at least lower than
30°F (-1°C)

(14)

4.

Drawings may vary.
But, angles should
have the following
measurements:
Angle 1: 45°;
Angle two: 80°;
Angle three: 30°;
Angle four: 15°;
Angle five: 135°;
Angle six: 150°

(12)

5.

Answers may vary.
Possible answers
include:

1. l = 2 in, w = 4 in,
   h = 8 in
2. l = 6 in, w = 4 in,
   h = 5 in
3. l = 9 in, w = 3 in,
   h = 3 in
4. l = 8 in, w = 5 in,
   h = 6 in
5. l = 5 in, w = 5 in,
   h = 6 in
6. l = 9 in, w = 2 in,
   h = 5 in
7. l = 13 cm,
   w = 23 cm, h = 8 cm
8. l = 20 cm,
   w = 10 cm, h = 10 cm
9. l = 18 cm, w = 8 cm,
   h = 25 cm
10. l = 15 cm,
    w = 25 cm, h = 20 cm
11. l = 10 cm,
    w = 18 cm, h = 15 cm

(13)

3.

a) 90°

b) 30°

c) 115°

d) 20°

e) 60°

f) 180°

g) 80°

(11)

2.

Answers may vary.
Students should list
items to scale or
1 inch = 1 foot or
1 cm = 10 cm.

(10)

1.

a)

442 m

391 m

381 m

374 m

355 m

344 m

319 m

312 m

310 m

299 m

(9)

14.

Answers may vary.

Students should come to realize that the volume of a rectangular prism is found by multiplying length x width x height.

Volume of a cylinder is found by finding the radius and using the following formula π x radius² x height.

The volume of a pyramid is found by multiplying ½ base x height.

(22)

13.

Formula one is for a right triangle

Formula two is for a rectangle, square, or parallelogram

Formula three is for a circle

Formula four is for a square

Student figures may vary.

(21)

11.

Answers may vary.

(19)

12.

a) $10.48

b) A small soft drink is 1/8 the cost of a chicken cutlet sandwich

c) Chicken cutlet, potato skins, large soft drink

d) $11.53

(20)

10.

380,000 lbs, 172,365 kg, 6,080,000 oz

160,000 lbs, 72,575 kg, 2,560,000 oz

70 tons, 140,000 lbs, 2,240,000 oz

65 tons, 130,000 lbs, 58,967 kg

7.5 tons, 6,803.9 kg, 240,000 oz

7,000 lbs, 3,175.1 kg, 112,000 oz

2.5 tons, 5,000 lbs, 80,000 oz

1.5 tons, 1,360.8 kg, 48,000 oz

2,500 lbs, 1,134 kg 40,000 oz

0.25 tons, 500 lbs, 226.8 kg

(18)

9.

a)

Circle One:
Circumference = 6.28 cm; Radius = 1 cm; Area = 3.14 sq. cm

b) Circle Two:
Circumference= 9.42 cm; Radius = 1.5 cm; Area = 7.065 sq. cm

c) Circle Three:
Circumference= 12.56 cm; Radius = 2 cm; Area = 12.56 sq. cm

(17)

8.

Year 1 = $.75 per quart ($0.40 per 500 ml)

Year 2 = $.76 per quart ($0.40 per 500 ml)

Year 3 = $.76 per quart ($0.41 per 500 ml)

Year 4 = $.79 per quart ($0.42 per 500 ml)

Year 5 = $.82 per quart ($0.44 per 500 ml)

Year 6 = $.86 per quart ($0.46 per 500 ml)

Year 7 = $.91 per quart ($0.48 per 500 ml)

Year 8 = $.96 per quart ($0.51 per 500 ml)

a) Students should recognize that the price increases by multiples of $0.03 per gallon (and an increase of $0.01 per liter), starting with year 1. Year 9 would increase 24 cents to become $4.07 per gallon (and increase 6 cents to become $1.07 per liter). Year 10 would increase 27 cents to become $4.34 per gallon (and increase 7 cents to become $1.14 per liter).

(16)

EZ ✓

15.

Cube 1 = .83 g/cm^3 (0.48 oz/in^3)

Cube 2 = .84 g/cm^3 (0.48 oz/in^3)

Cube 3 = .77 g/cm^3 (0.45 oz/in^3)

Cube 4 = .79 g/cm^3 (0.46 oz/in^3)

Cube 5 = .83 g/cm^3 (0.48 oz/in^3)

Cube 6 = .94 g/cm^3 (0.54 oz/in^3)

Cube 7 = .80 g/cm^3 (0.46 oz/in^3)

Cube 8 = .86 g/cm^3 (0.50 oz/in^3)

Cube 9 = .82 g/cm^3 (0.48 oz/in^3)

Cube 10 = .87 g/cm^3 (0.50 oz/in^3)

Drill Sheet 1

a) 150 cm
7 yards
15 ft
.16 lbs
2500 mg
500 lbs
2 pints
.33kL
8 quarts
6 yds
2500 m
972 in

b) A = 60 sq. cm
P = 32 cm

c) A = 10.5 sq. in
P = 21 in

d) A = 16 sq. m
P = 16 m

e) 60 cubic feet (1.8 cubic meters)

f) 192°F (80°C)

g) 72°

h) A = πr^2

i) 5000 m (15,840 feet)

Drill Sheet 2

a) 45 ft
20 cm
7.5 ft
.9 kg
30 lbs
4000 lbs
1.25 gallons
2 quarts
.16 L
9000 m
366 in
5000 mm

b) 135°
c) 45°
d) 165°

e) 25 sq. cm (4 sq. in)

f) diameter

g) 250 sq. ft. (20 sq. m)

h) 15 inches (39 cm)

i) 50 miles (80 km)

Review A

a) 126,720 in; 3520 yd. 2 miles

6,000,000 mm; 600,000 cm; 6 km

16,000 oz; .5 ton

64 cups; 32 pints; 4 gallons

b) Figures may vary.

c) Answers may vary. Students should recognize that the area of a rectangle is found by determining length and width, then multiplying the two measurements. The perimeter is the measurement of all sides and is found by adding both lengths to both widths.

Review B

a) 158,400 in; 13,200 ft; 4400 yd

3,500,000 mm; 350,000 cm; 3500 m

128,000 oz; 8000 lbs

80 cups; 40 pints; 20 quarts

b) Figures may vary.

c) Answers may vary. Students should realize that the length, width, and height of the rectangular prism are needed. By multiplying the three measurements, students will find the volume, labeled in cubic measurements.

Review C

a) 44,352 in; 3696 ft; 1232 yd

35,000 mm; 35 m; .035 km

1000 lb, 0.5 ton

8 pints; 4 quarts; 1 gallon

b) Figures may vary.

c) Answers may vary. Students should recognize that they have to find the area of the top and bottom circles found on a cylinder by using the formula π x radius^2 for each circle. Then, they need to find the area of the remainder of the cylinder, called the side, using the formula 2 x π x radius x height. The final formula is $2\pi r^2 + 2\pi rh$.

EZ✓

6.

Answers may vary.

(6A)

5.

a) 96 sq. cm (24 sq. in)

b) 4400 quarts (4,162,750 ml)

c) 78.5 sq. cm (12.56 sq. in)

d) 6.05 mph (9.75 kph) or .1 mpm

e) 750 sq. ft (70 sq. m)

f) 60 °

g) 60 mm (2.45 in)

h) 21 in (54 cm)

(5A)

4.

a) 50.24 sq. cm (7.07 sq. in)

b) 260 gallons (988 liters)

c) 35°

d) 60,000 m (190,080 feet)

e) 1728 in³ (27000 cm³)

f) 52.875 feet

g) 185 oz(5700 g) or 11.56 lbs (5.28 kg)

(4A)

3.

a) 3 gallons (she will have 2 quarts extra) (9 liters)

b) 1170 miles (1883 km)

c) 40 inches (104 cm)

d) 3 tons (6,000 pounds)

e) 120 °

f) 144°F (80°C)

g) 8 cm (3 in)

(3A)

2.

a) 40,000 pounds (18,140 kg)

b) - 20°C (12°F)

c) 14 sq. inches (90 sq. cm)

d) 5 percent

e) 624 gallons (2340 liters)

f) 50.767 seconds

(2A)

1.

a) 3000 lbs
96 oz
6 tons
50 mm
2500 m
18.2cm
.08 kL
2.5 gallons
12 cups
60 in
7.5ft
270 in

b) Pictures should look like angles described.

c) i) 26 cm (10 in)

ii) 35°F (2°C)

iii) diameter

iv)10 sq. in. (65 sq. cm)

(1A)

Measurement – Task & Drill Sheets CC3315

6.

a)
i) 2.5 miles = 13200 feet, 158,400 in
ii) 8250 in = 687.5 feet, 0.13 miles
iii) 10,000 ft = 1.89 miles, 120,000 in
iv) 26.2 miles = 138336 ft, 1,660,032 in
v) 22,500 in = 0.36 miles, 1875 ft
vi) 12,580 ft = 2.38 miles, 150,960 in
vii) 27.4 miles = 144,672 ft, 1,736,064 in
viii) 82.5 m = 8,250 cm, 82,500 mm
ix) 18.3 km = 18,300 m, 1,830,000 cm
x) 156 cm = 1.56 m, 1,560 mm
xi) 1258 m = 1.258 km, 125,800 cm
xii) 8276.7 m = 8.276 m, 827.67 cm
xiii) 413.7 m = 413,700 cm, 4,137,000 mm
xiv) 92.5 km = 92,500 m, 9,250,000 cm
xv) 275.5 cm = 2.755 m, 2755 mm
xvi) 328.5 m = 0.3285 km, 328,500 cm
xvii) 23,000 ft = 4.4 miles, 276,000 in
xviii) 97 miles = 6,145,910 in, 512,160 ft
xix) 0.03 km = 3000 cm, 30 m
xx) 250,000 mm = 250 m, 25,000 cm

5.

a)
i) 8.64 sq in (54 sq cm)
ii) 15.36 sq in (96 sq cm)
iii) 486 sq in (3174 sq cm)
iv) 6 sq in (37.5 sq cm)
v) 24 sq in (150 sq cm)
vi) 54 sq in (346.56 sq cm)
vii) 132.54 sq in (864 sq cm)
viii) 19.44 sq in (121.5 sq cm)
ix) 37.5 sq in (245.76 sq cm)

b)
i) 2.8 in (7 cm)
ii) 4 in (10 cm)
iii) 4.7 in (12 cm)
iv) 4.3 in (11 cm)
v) 7.9 in (20 cm)
vi) 7 in (18 cm)
vii) 9.8 in (25 cm)
viii) 13 in (33 cm)

4.

a)
i) 17 in (42.5 cm), 34 in (85 cm)
ii) 6.5 in (17 cm), 13 in (34 cm)
iii) 6.1 in (15 cm), 12.2 in (30 cm)
iv) 21 in (53.3 cm), 42 in (106.6 cm)
v) 10.3 in (25.5 cm), 20.6 in (510 cm)
vi) 7.3 in (18.5 cm), 14.6 in (37 cm)
vii) 8.4 in (21.5 cm), 16.8 in (43 cm)
viii) 18 in (45.3 cm), 36 in (90.6 cm)
ix) 4.8 in (11.5 cm), 9.6 in (23 cm)
x) 7.3 in (18.5 cm), 14.6 in (37 cm)
xi) 19 in (48 cm), 38 in (96 cm)
xii) 9.9 in (25.5 cm), 19.8 in (51 cm)
xiii) 8.5 in (21.5 cm), 17 in (43 cm)
xiv) 13.5 in (34 cm), 27 in (68 cm)
xv) 27 in (68.5 cm), 54 in (137 cm)

3.

a)
i) Area = 1.2 sq in (8 sq cm), Perimeter = 4.6 in (12 cm)
ii) Area = 20.25 sq in (144 sq cm), Perimeter = 18 in (48 cm)
iii) Area = 1.2 sq in (7.5 sq cm), Perimeter = 6 in (15 cm)
iv) Area = 30.25 sq in (196 sq cm), Perimeter = 22 in (56 cm)
v) Area = 10.5 sq in (65.625 sq cm), Perimeter = 20 in (50.5 cm)
vi) Area = 7.5 sq in (48.75 sq cm), Perimeter = 11 in (28 cm)
vii) Area = 12 sq in (80 sq cm), Perimeter = 14 in (36 cm)
viii) Area = 32.5 sq in (210.375 sq cm), Perimeter = 26 in (62 cm)
ix) Area = 13.5 sq in (96 sq cm), Perimeter = 15 in (40 cm)

2.

a)
i) 3 quarts
ii) 15 gallons
iii) 5 cups
iv) 2.25 gallons
v) 50 quarts
vi) 32 cups
vii) 5.5 gallons
viii) 72 pints
ix) 65 cups
x) 3.75 gallons
xi) 7.25 quarts
xii) 29 quarts
xiii) 39 pints

b)
i) 0.002 kL
ii) 0.05 L
iii) 0.3 kL
iv) 9500 L
v) 32500 mL
vi) 2500000 mL
vii) 500 mL
viii) 0.0026 kL
ix) 5.216 kL
x) 1.3 L
xi) 0.05026 kL
xii) 8,230,000 mL
xiii) 75 L
xiv) 22 L
xv) 0.0185 kL

1.

a)
Answers will vary. Make sure the student chooses 3 items for each combo, the total amount includes the 5% sales tax, and the change received from a $10.00 is correct.

7.

a)

i) A = 1734 sq in (18.84 sq cm),
C = 14.76 in (37.68 cm)

ii) A = 7.065 sq in (44.16 sq cm),
C = 9.42 in (23.55 cm)

iii) A = 4.52 sq in (28.26 sq cm),
C = 7.54 in (18.84 cm)

iv) A = 78.5 sq in (506.45 sq cm),
C = 31.4 in (79.76 cm)

v) A = 140.96 sq in (907.46 sq cm),
C = 42.08 in (106.76 cm)

vi) A = 9.62 sq in (63.59 sq cm),
C = 10.99 in (28.26 cm)

vii) A = 78.5 sq in (510.45 sq cm),
C = 31.4 in (80.07 cm)

viii) A = 2.54 sq in (15.9 sq cm),
C = 5.65 in (14.13 cm)

ix) A = 167.33 sq in (1074.67 sq cm),
C = 45.84 in (116.18 cm)

x) A = 1766.25 sq in (1133.54 sq cm),
C = 47.1 in (119.32 cm)

xi) A = 248.72 sq in (1589.63 sq cm),
C = 55.89 in (141.3 cm)

xii) A = 0.79 sq in (4.91 sq cm),
C = 3.14 in (7.85 cm)

xiii) A = 15.9 sq in (103.82 sq cm),
C = 14.13 in (36.11 cm)

xiv) A = 415.27 sq in (2686.47 sq cm),
C = 72.22 in (183.69 cm)

xv) A = 113.04 sq in (735.05 sq cm),
C = 37.68 in (96.1 cm)

xvi) A = 12.56 sq in (78.5 sq cm),
C = 12.56 in (31.4 cm)

xvii) A = 153.86 sq in (994.88 sq cm),
C = 43.96 in (111.78 cm)

8.

a)

i) 4.81 (2.96),
0.08 (0.049)

ii) 4.94 (3.04),
0.082 (0.051)

iii) 4.99 (3.07),
0.083 (0.051)

iv) 5.05 (3.11),
0.084 (0.052)

v) 5.11 (3.15),
0.085 (0.053)

vi) 5.12 (3.15),
0.085 (0.053)

vii) 5.12 (3.15),
0.085 (0.053)

viii) 5.13 (3.16),
0.086 (0.053)

ix) 5.19 (3.19),
0.087 (0.053)

x) 5.25 (3.23),
0.088 (0.054)

xi) 5.28 (3.25),
0.088 (0.054)

xii) 5.58 (3.43),
0.093 (0.057)

xiii) 5.59 (3.44),
0.093 (0.057)

xiv) 5.62 (3.46),
0.094 (0.058)

xv) 5.75 (3.54),
0.096 (0.059)

9.

a)

i) Triangle or
Parallelogram

ii) Triangle

iii) Quadrilateral

iv) Pentagon

v) Circle

vi) Quadrilateral

vii) Square

viii) Hexagon

ix) Cube

Shapes will vary.
Areas and Perimeters
will vary.

10.

a)

i) Perimeter = 5.2 in
(12 cm),
Area = 1.69 sq in
(9 sq cm)

ii) Perimeter = 4.2 in
(10 cm),
Area = 1.04 sq in
(6 sq cm)

iii) Perimeter = 4 in
(10 cm),
Area = 1 sq in
(6.25 sq cm)

iv) Perimeter = 5.2 in
(12 cm),
Area = 4.4 sq in
(10.6 sq cm)

v) Perimeter = 3 in
(7.4 cm),
Area = 0.28 sq in
(1.7 sq cm)

vi) Perimeter = 5.2 in
(13 cm),
Area = 1.6 sq in
(10 sq cm)

vii) Answers will vary.

viii) Answers will vary.

11.

Answers may vary.

12.

a)

i) 12 ft = 144 in

ii) 0.5 yd = 1.5 ft

iii) 72 in = 2 yds

iv) 7.5 ft = 2.5 yds

v) 2.5 yds = 90 in

vi) 21 ft = 252 in

vii) 78 in = 6.5 ft

viii) 30 yds = 1080 in

ix) 3.3 yd = 118.8 in

x) 42 in = 3.5 ft

xi) 16 in = 1.3 ft

xii) 26.5 yds = 79.5 ft

xiii) 3 m = 3,000 mm

xiv) 2.5 cm = 250 mm

xv) 19 cm = 190 mm

xvi) 14 m = 1400 cm

xvii) 855 mm = 0.855 m

xviii) 9.5 cm = 0.095 m

xix) 326 mm = 32.6 cm

xx) 29 cm = 290 mm

xxi) 25 cm = 0.25 m

xxii) 1890 mm = 189 cm

13.

a)

i) 22 sq in (137.5 sq cm)

ii) 184 sq in (1150 sq cm)

iii) 192 sq in (1200 sq cm)

iv) 117 sq in (765 sq cm)

v) 324 sq in (2025 sq cm)

vi) 9.5 sq in (58 sq cm)

vii) 1398 sq in (8969 sq cm)

viii) 27 sq in (175 sq cm)

ix) 802 sq in (5118 sq cm)

x) 300 sq in (1924 sq cm)

xi) 216 sq in (1350 sq cm)

xii) 192 sq in (1200 sq cm)

xiii) 304 sq in (1900 sq cm)

xiv) 52 sq in (325 sq cm)

xv) 365 sq in (2334 sq cm)

xvi) 51.5 sq in (328 sq cm)

xvii) 5.5 sq in (33 sq cm)

xviii) 351 sq in (2250 sq cm)

xix) 184.5 sq in (1148 sq cm)

xx) 220 sq in (1387.5 sq cm)

35   36   37   38   39   40   41

Review C

a)
i) 18.3 yd = ~~~ (partially obscured)
ii) 1.28 cm = 12.8 mm
iii) 0.25 tons = 500 lbs
iv) 1.025 m = 1025 mm
v) 198 oz = 12.375 lbs
vi) 7.5 g = 7500 kg
vii) 144 qt = 36 gallons
viii) 1.25 km = 125,000 cm
ix) 40.3 ft = 483.6 in
x) 27.55 kg = 27,550 g
xi) 24.5 ft = 8.16 yds
xii) 4.25 km = 4250 m
xiii) 25.25 g = 25,250 mg
xiv) 8.25 ft = 99 in
xv) 0.028 kL = 28 L

b)
i) 16.76 seconds
ii) Answers may vary.
iii) 75.75 miles = 399,960 feet
(121.8 km = 121,800 meters)
iv) 20 sq in (132 sq cm)
v) 78.5 sq in (490.625 sq cm)

c)
i) Base = 0.8 in (2 cm),
Side = 1.4 in (3.5 cm),
Height = 1.4 in (3.5 cm),
Area = 1.12 sq in (7 sq cm),
Perimeter = 4.4 in (11 cm)
ii) Radius = 0.5 in (1.4 cm),
Area = 0.8 sq in (6.2 sq cm),
Circumference = 3.14 in
(8.8 cm)
iii) Side = 0.8 in (2 cm),
Area = 0.64 sq in (4 sq cm),
Perimeter = 3.2 in (8 cm)

48

Review B

a)
i) 2.57 cm = 25.7 mm
ii) 4.5 ft = 54 in
iii) 12.5 gal = 200 cups
iv) 5.5 km = 550,000 cm
v) 24 oz = 1.5 lbs
vi) 0.5 kL = 500 L
vii) 138 in = 11.5 ft
viii) 175 mm = 17.5 cm
ix) 30 qt = 7.5 gallons
x) 19.27 mg = 0.01927 g
xi) 28.5 oz = 1.78 lbs
xii) 29.25 kg = 292,500 g
xiii) 22.5 ft = 270 in
xiv) 0.025 kL = 2.5 L
xv) 2.5 tons = 80,000 oz

b)
i) -19.4°C
ii) 2.4 inches (6.1 cm)
iii) 1364 oz (38670 grams)
iv) 52.8 miles (85 km)
v) 15 cubic inches
(280 cubic cm)

c)
i) Base = 0.5 in (1.5 cm),
Side = 1.2 in (3 cm),
Perimeter = 2.9 in (7.5 cm)
ii) Diameter = 1 in (2.5 cm),
Circumference = 3.14 in
(7.85 cm)
iii) Base = 1 in (2.5 cm),
Side = 1 in (2.5 cm),
Perimeter = 4 in (10 cm)

47

Review A

a)
i) 20 ft = 240 in
ii) 480 mm = 48 cm
iii) 176 oz = 11 lbs
iv) 500 m = 0.5 km
v) 72 ft = 24 yd
vi) 7.5 kL = 7500 L
vii) 128 qts = 32 gallons
viii) 2.5 m = 250 cm
ix) 45 ft = 15 yd
x) 7 km = 7,000,000 mm
xi) 4.5 cup = 2.25 pt
xii) 12 L = 12,000 mL
xiii) 18.5 ft = 222 in
xiv) 29.7 g = 29,700 mg
xv) 25 lbs = 400 oz

b)
i) 64.5°F (14.5°C)
ii) Answers may vary.
iii) 26,400 feet (8000 meters)
iv) 5000 pounds
(2268 kilograms)
v) 3 sq in (1912.5 sq mm)
vi) 14 in (36 cm)

c)
i) Base = 1.2 in (3 cm),
Height = 1.4 in (3.5 cm),
Area = 0.84 sq in (5.25 sq cm)
ii) Side = 1.2 inches (3 cm),
Area = 1.44 sq in (9 sq cm)
iii) Length = 1 in (2.5 cm),
Height = 1.2 in (3 cm),
Area = 1.2 sq in (7.5 sq cm)

46

17.

a)
i) Surface Area = 40 sq in
(250 sq cm),
Volume = 16 cu in
(250 cu cm)
ii) Surface Area = 27.5 sq in
(174 sq cm),
Volume = 8.4 cu in
(135 cu cm)
iii) Surface Area = 77.5 sq in
(506.36 sq cm),
Volume = 43.75 cu in
(731.52 cu cm)
iv) Surface Area = 17 sq in
(111 sq cm),
Volume = 4.2 cu in
(70 cu cm)
v) Surface Area = 258.5 sq in
(1661.44 sq cm),
Volume = 267.75 cu in
(4362.78 cu cm)
vi) Surface Area = 3.92 sq in
(27 sq cm),
Volume = 0.48 cu in
(9 cu cm)
vii) Surface Area = 146.5 sq in
(951.2 sq cm),
Volume = 115.5 cu in
(1915.2 cu cm)
viii) Surface Area = 61.44 sq in
(384 sq cm),
Volume = 32.77 cu in
(512 cu cm)
ix) Surface Area = 167.5 sq in
(1072 sq cm),
Volume = 143 cu in
(2310 cu cm)
x) Surface Area = 46 sq in
(287.5 sq cm),
Volume = 20.4 cu in
(318.75 cu cm)
xi) Surface Area = 400 sq in
(2562.1 sq cm),
Volume = 456 cu in
(7350.5 cu cm)
xii) Surface Area = 38.92 sq in
(247.5 sq cm),
Volume = 13.72 cu in
(218.75 cu cm)

45

15.

Shapes will vary.

43

16.

a)
i) 43.75 miles (72 km)
ii) 56.25 miles (91.2 km)
iii) 62.5 miles (102.4 km)
iv) 68.75 miles (112 km)
v) 81.25 miles (132.8 km)
vi) 87.5 miles (142.4 km)
vii) 93.75 miles (152 km)
viii) 100 miles (163.2 km)
ix) 103.75 miles (168 km)
x) 106.25 miles (172.8 km)
xi) 112.5 miles (182.4 km)
xii) 118.75 miles (192 km)
xiii) 125 miles (203.2 km)
xiv) 130 miles (211.2 km)
xv) 137.5 miles (224 km)
xvi) 143.75 miles (233.6 km)
xvii) 155 miles (252.8 km)
xviii) 156.25 miles (254.4 km)
xix) 168.75 miles (275.2 km)
xx) 187.5 miles (304 km)

44

14.

a)
i) Monday = 17.3°F
(9.6°C)
Tuesday = 20.4°F
(11.3°C)
Wednesday = 25.4°F
(14.1°C)
Thursday = 18.1°F
(10.1°C)
Friday = 17.9°F (9.9°C)

ii) 76.36°F (24.64°C)
iii) 56.54°F (13.64°C)
iv) Monday = 66.95°F
(19.4°C)
Tuesday = 67°F
(19.45°C)
Wednesday = 65.2°F
(18.45°C)
Thursday = 69.35°F
(20.75°C)
Friday = 63.75°F
(17.65°C)

v) Wednesday
vi) Monday
vii) 25.9°F (14.4°C)

42

(these answers are for the 6 free bonus pages, see page 5 for download instructions)

EZ✔

1.

a)

i) 4 in (10.2 cm)

ii) 1800 in (4570 cm)

iii) 6 in (15.23 cm)

iv) 1.19 in (3 cm)

v) 22 quarts (22 liters)

vi) 18.8 in (48 cm)

vii) 3.14 sq in (19.6 sq cm)

viii) 2.43 in (6 cm)

ix) 1.83 in (12 cm)

x) 33°F (7°C)

xi) 216 inches (550 cm)

xii) 20 feet (6.16 meters)

xiii) 20 minutes

xiv) 19.7 feet (6 meters)

xv) 5 miles (8.045 km)

1A

2.

a)

Answers will vary.

2A

3.

a)

i) 30 lbs (13.6 kg)

ii) 83.3 lbs (37.8 kg)

iii) 15 lbs (6.8 kg)

iv) 75 lbs (34.02 kg)

v) 366.7 lbs (166.32 kg)

vi) 23.3 lbs (10.58 kg)

vii) 3.33 lbs (1.52 kg)

viii) 1333.33 lbs (604.78 kg)

ix) 300 lbs (136.08 kg)

x) 750 lbs (340.2 kg)

xi) 3 lbs (1.37 kg)

xii) 16.67 lbs (7.57 kg)

xiii) 66.67 lbs (30.23 kg)

xiv) 1.67 lbs (0.75 kg)

xv) 3.5 lbs (1.58 kg)

xvi) 666.67 lbs (302.4 kg)

xvii) 100 lbs (45.37 kg)

xviii) 50 lbs (22.68 kg)

xix) 4.17 lbs (1.88 kg)

xx) 133.33 lbs (60.48 kg)

3A

4.

a)

Answers will vary. Paragraphs should explain that a person must determine the lengths of each side and add them together to find the perimeter. A person needs to determine the height. The person multiplies the height by the length of the base and divides by two to find the area. Area is measured in square units while perimeter is measured in units.

The base of the triangle is 4.1 inches (10.5 cm), the side lengths are 3 inches (7.5 cm), and the height is 2.1 inches (5.3 cm). The area of the triangle is 4.3 square inches (27.8 square cm). The perimeter of the triangle is 10.1 inches (25.5 cm).

4A

5.

a)

i) 18°F = -7.78°C

ii) 25°F = -3.89°C

iii) 47°F = 8.33°C

iv) 84°F = 28.89°C

v) 160°F = 71.11°C

vi) -4°F = -20°C

vii) 320°F = 160°C

viii) 188°F = 86.67°C

ix) 270°F = 132.22°C

x) -40°F = -40°C

xi) 99°F = 37.22°C

xii) 318°F = 158.89°C

xiii) 72°F = 22.22°C

xiv) -100°F = -73.33°C

xv) 450°F = 232.22°C

xvi) 800°F = 426.67°C

xvii) 325°F = 162.78°C

xviii) 56°F = 13.33°C

b)

i) 12°C = 53.6°F

ii) 80°C = 176°F

iii) 101°C = 213.8°F

iv) 92°C = 197.6°F

v) -5°C = 23°F

vi) 200°C = 392°F

vii) 120°C = 248°F

viii) 45°C = 113°F

ix) -18°C = -0.4°F

x) 47°C = 116.6°F

xi) 290°C = 554°F

xii) 32°C = 89.6°F

xiii) 158°C = 316.4°F

xiv) 492°C = 917.6°F

xv) -27°C = -16.6°F

xvi) 44°C = 111.2°F

xvii) -9°C = 15.8°F

xviii) 188°C = 370.4°F

5A

6.

a)

i) Area = 7.5 sq in (46.9 sq cm). Perimeter = 11 in (27.5 cm)

ii) Area = 3 sq in (20 sq cm). Perimeter = 7 in (18 cm)

iii) Area = 1.44 sq in (9 sq cm). Perimeter = 4.8 in (12 cm)

iv) Area = 12.56 sq in (78.5 sq cm). Circumference = 12.56 in (31.4 cm)

v) Area = 2 sq in (12 sq cm). Perimeter = 6.6 in (16 cm)

vi) Area = 9 sq in (56.25 sq cm). Perimeter = 17 in (42.5 cm)

vii) Area = 2.86 sq in (19.25 sq cm). Perimeter = 7 in (18 cm)

viii) Area = 7.5 sq in (45 sq cm). Perimeter = 14 in (35 cm)

ix) Area = 4.48 sq in (28 sq cm). Perimeter = 8.8 in (22 cm)

x) Area = 42.25 sq in (272.25 sq cm). Perimeter = 26 in (66 cm)

xi) Area = 1.33 sq in (1.53 sq cm). Circumference = 4.08 in (10.99 cm)

xii) Area = 10.5 sq in (63.75 sq cm). Perimeter = 13 in (32 cm)

6A

Money, Money, Money

You have been assigned to work with a design committee to create a new denomination of coin or bill. Your task is to complete the following tasks as you prepare to release the newest denomination within the year.

a) Determine which new denomination of coin or bill would be useful to the public.

b) Create a name for this new denomination.

c) Explain why this new denomination would be beneficial to consumers.

d) Select a person to appear on the front of the new coin or bill. This person should be a figure from history who had a positive impact. Explain why this person should appear on a unit of currency.

e) Design the new coin or bill and how it would look.

f) Unveil the new design for your classmates. Show ten ways it can be combined with other denominations to make change (for example if you invented the nickel, $1.00 + a nickel = $1.05).

Draw it to Scale

You have been hired by the Scholastic Architectural Firm to design a new classroom. Your job is to draw the design of your state-of-the-art classroom, complete with tools that you think will be useful for students in your class or grade. For this, you are asked to do the following:

a) Design a floor space for your classroom on a regular piece of white paper. Explain the scale of your drawing (for example 1 inch (1 cm) in your drawing might equal 1 foot (1 meter)).

b) Identify the area and perimeter of the classroom you have designed.

c) Add at least three pieces of furniture to your classroom (you do not need to put student desks in your design, but do need to have an area for it). Label the furniture and draw it to scale.

d) Draw three educational tools that will be incorporated in the floor design. Label the items and draw it to scale.

e) Explain why your new classroom would be an innovation over current classrooms.

f) Add the scale to your drawing.

Time's Up

For this task you will need either a stopwatch or a clock with a minute hand. Your job is to work under the supervision of an adult and to determine a task that everyone in a small group might be able to do (recite a poem, read a passage from a story, do the twelve times table). After you do this:

a) Time each person in your group performing the task. Record the times on a piece of paper. Denote the number of minutes and/or seconds it takes. This is called the first trial.

b) Complete the task again now that all members have done it once. This is called the second trial. See how the times change now that each group member has some practice.

c) Place the times onto a double bar chart representing each participant so times can be compared. Place the names in order from shortest to longest based on the times during the second trial.

d) Make a list of at least ten observations about the difference in times on the chart from the first trial to the second trial.

e) Summarize your findings and share them in class.

Area of a Circle

Look at the picture of the circle below. Discuss how you can determine the area and perimeter of the circle. Then, in a well developed paragraph, explain how to find the area.
Finally, measure the circle and find the area and perimeter.

Things to consider in your answer:

1. What measurements will you need?
2. What units of measure will you use?
3. How do the measurements you need relate to each other?

Things to consider in your paragraph:

1. Make sure to include a topic sentence and conclusion.
2. Make sure your paragraph contains at least five sentences.
3. Make sure to use transition words to help explain your work.

To Scale

Think about the layout of your school. In small groups, draw a map of your entire school to scale. If possible, work with others to determine the perimeter measurements of your school, as well as interior measurements. Then, working with a teacher or adult, complete the following.

– Select a scale in which to draw your map. For example, 1 inch (1 cm) on your map may equal 10 feet (1.2 meters) in your school. Label the scale on your drawing.
– Draw the perimeter of your school first. Make sure to label the perimeter on your map.
– Draw interior rooms on your map.
– Label the area of your school.
– Identify your classroom. Label the area of your classroom.
– Label important structures in your school.
– Find the perimeter of another room in your school. Make sure you have permission first.

When done, compare your drawings with those of your classmates. Which scale was easiest to work with? Which scale was most difficult? What complications arose in the development of the map?

First, as a class, draw the layout of your classroom below.

Surface Area of a Rectangular Prism

Obtain a box or other rectangular prism. Working alone or in a small group, devise a plan to determine the surface area of the box without measuring any of the sides.

Then, do the following.

1. Explain your plan.

_____

_____

2. Test your plan. Did it work? _____

3. Take measurements of your box. Make sure to identify the main measurements needed for your box. _____

4. Calculate the surface area of the box. _____

5. Compare the surface area you determined by your calculations to the surface area you determined by using your plan. _____

_____

6. Write your findings in a well organized paragraph.

_____

_____

_____

_____

_____

_____

7. Draw a diagram of your box. Label all of the essential measurements you took to determine the surface area.